INDEPENDENT BUSES AROUND STOKE-ON-TRENT

CLIFF BEETON

AMBERLEY

First published 2023

Amberley Publishing
The Hill, Stroud
Gloucestershire, GL5 4EP

www.amberley-books.com

ISBN 978 1 3981 1365 7 (print)
ISBN 978 1 3981 1366 4 (ebook)

British Library Cataloguing in Publication Data.
A catalogue record for this book is available from the British Library.

Origination by Amberley Publishing.
Printed in the UK.

Introduction

My last book looked at Potteries Motor Traction, the dominant operator in the area from National Bus Company days in 1980 until the current Firstbus operation in 2020. We will take a look at the plethora of interesting independent bus operators that have provided bus services alongside PMT during the same period, covering Stoke-on-Trent, Newcastle-under-Lyme and the surrounding areas including neighbouring towns such as Crewe, Congleton, Leek, Stafford and Uttoxeter, which were also served by PMT.

In 1980 the well-established Potteries area independents Stoniers of Goldenhill, Berresfords of Cheddleton, Turner's of Brown Edge and Procters of Hanley were all running double-deckers into Hanley daily, some of these vehicles having been purchased new. Working alongside the double-deckers on other routes were a multitude of single-deckers of varying age and pedigree. Crossing over to Newcastle-under-Lyme, Pooles Coachways of Alsagers Bank worked services westwards to Silverdale, Park Site, Halmerend and Audley using bus-bodied Leyland Leopard and AEC Reliance single-deckers that were mostly purchased new.

The yellow buses of Stevensons of Uttoxeter tended to work services in the south of the area around Uttoxeter but they became more common in the Potteries after Stevensons purchased the Crystal Coaches operation at Hassel Street, Newcastle-under-Lyme, in September 1984 and later relocated this operation to larger new premises in Nevada Lane on the Hot Lane industrial estate in Burslem. Stevensons was sold to British Bus in 1994, later merging with Cowie to become Arriva.

Following local bus service deregulation in October 1986, Stoniers, Berresfords and Turner's were all sold to the ever-expanding PMT in 1987. Pooles Coachways nearly joined them as they were in the process of being sold to Berresfords Motors, but the deal had not been signed before proprietor Jim Berresford's premature death in 1987. Pooles Coachways were subsequently sold to McCreadys shortly afterwards, but didn't last too long before eventually passing to PMT.

Knotty Bus and Coach of Chesterton started operations in 1988 using a fleet of interesting older vehicles of mainly AEC parentage, including Swifts and Reliances, on local services around the Potteries. Following a depot fire and subsequent sale it fell by the wayside shortly afterwards.

D&G Bus started with a handful of minibuses working Stoke-on-Trent City Council-tendered services from part of the old PMT Longton depot. It later expanded and opened new depots in Mossfield Road, Longton, and at Crewe. The Longton depot and routes were sold to Arriva-owned Wardle Transport in 2011 but repurchased again in 2015. Further expansion and acquisitions have seen D&G Bus become the largest independent operator in the area after First Potteries before being sold to Centrebus in 2019.

Local coach operators also tried their hand at running buses. Bakers of Biddulph started with a handful of minibuses and had later expanded to such an extent that it eventually ran more buses than coaches. It became the dominant operator in Biddulph running from that town to Hanley, Newcastle, Stafford, Leek, and Congleton, eventually reaching Macclesfield and even Stockport. Perhaps the high point was the purchase of three Wright Gemini-bodied Volvo B5H hybrid double-deckers in 2011 before looming financial problems saw drastic cuts to the bus services and the fleet before being sold to Island Fortitude in August 2013. A continued steady decline followed before the remaining bus services and a handful of buses were purchased by D&G Bus in January 2015, with the rest of Bakers eventually passing into oblivion a few years later.

Scraggs of Bucknall also started running buses under the 'Blue Buses' fleetname from Hanley to Ball Green, Newcastle, Abbey Hulton and Werrington after deregulation. They outgrew the old Bucknall premises and later relocated to a new garage at Adderley Green. Today they still run on the Hanley–Abbey Hulton route.

Copelands of Meir registered local bus service 40 between Longton and Fenton via Heron Cross after deregulation, initially using minibuses and later purchasing a pair of ex-PMT Plaxton Pointer-bodied Dennis Darts. They also ran Sunday tendered journeys on the 16 from Leek to Hanley for a while. Copelands route 40 passed to D&G Bus in 2016.

Matthews Motors Handy Bus ran a fleet of mainly old minibuses around Newcastle-under-Lyme to areas formerly served by Pooles. They also had some larger vehicles, including two Bristol LHs and a Seddon. They would later purchase the former Crystal Coaches operations at Burslem from Arriva that had previously been the Stevensons operation in the Potteries.

RML Travel started operations between Hanley and Birches Head in competition with PMT in 2006, later expanding onto a second route 41 serving Stoke, the hospital and Westbury Park. After only a couple of years operation the routes and a handful of buses passed to D&G Bus in 2009.

Wardle Transport started bus operations in 2004 using three ex-Hong Kong tri-axle Leyland Olympians on school work and later expanded to provide Stoke City FC buses and council-tendered bus services. It was sold to Arriva Midlands in 2010.

Long-established Procters of Hanley suddenly ceased trading in early March 2013, just short of its centenary, with Wardle Transport taking over the 16 Leek–Hanley service.

Over in Crewe, Best Bus ran a short-lived service to Nantwich, while D&G Bus, GHA Coaches, Mikro and Routemaster Buses between them gradually established themselves on the tendered services once run by PMT from its depot in the town.

Stantons of Stoke is one of the newer players on the local bus scene in the Potteries. It was formed in 2014 to take over the former Wardle Transport welfare buses from Arriva, later expanding into local bus work. It also works buses for Stoke City FC away fans.

Midland Classic of Burton purchased the Burton-on-Trent garage from Arriva Midlands in 2016 along with the bus services and some vehicles and now runs into Uttoxeter from Burton. Most of these services were former Stevensons services. Midland Classic was later sold to Rotala in August 2022.

GHA Coaches of Ruabon had expanded into Congleton and Crewe by winning council-tendered work. New buses were purchased in 2015 for the Beartown network and the 42 Crewe–Congleton service, but GHA later collapsed in 2016. Retendering by Cheshire East Council saw D&G win the 42 and local coach operator Hollinsheads of Biddulph win the two bus Beartown network.

In November 2020 D&G Bus purchased the Cannock depot and the routes it operated from Arriva Midlands, along with fifty-seven buses. These buses were painted into D&G Bus red livery but run under the Chaserider brand. Some of the Stafford Town services run by Chaserider were later transferred to associated company Select Bus Services to run.

Other operators that were based outside the area, but ran into it, are also shown to add to the variety of vehicles on offer.

Choosing which photos to include in a book is always a difficult proposition; with a collection of over forty years of interesting pictures at hand there is always something that has to be left out as there is inevitably not enough space to include everything. Some vehicles are included twice as they have worked for more than one operator locally or are shown in different liveries.

This book is not designed to be a comprehensive record of every bus and operator that has worked in the area, but acts as a tribute to those that I managed to catch over the last forty-or-so years.

Aimees of Leek operated this Wadham Stringer-bodied Leyland Swift E993 NMK (No. 29) in their attractive pink and white livery. It was new to Armchair Passenger Services of Brentford and later worked locally for Stevensons of Spath. It is seen here leaving the old Hanley bus station on a Sunday council-tendered service on the 16 Hanley–Leek.

The only full-sized single-decker bus in the Aimees of Leek fleet was this Alexander Dennis Enviro 300 GW55 SON (No. 29) seen here on the parking area adjacent to the garage at Leek lettered up for the 319 Ipstones–Leek service on 20 January 2014. It was new to Glyn Williams of Llanelli.

The first full-sized bus in the Bakers of Biddulph fleet was Plaxton Verde-bodied Volvo B10B M875 NWK (No. 164) that had been new as a Volvo demonstrator in May 1995. It initially received the Bakers attractive white and green coach livery, as seen here at Bakers Spring Grove garage in summer 2003. It would later receive the yellow and blue livery.

Bakers were allocated three Cheshire County Council-owned Wright Cadet-bodied DAF SB 120s for use on the council-contracted routes 26 and 27 between Macclesfield and Knutsford, but they occasionally strayed onto other routes. Here is YJ04 BZD in Cheshire Rider livery leaving Congleton for Biddulph.

Bakers purchased three brand new Wright Cadet-bodied DAF SB120s for the X1 Hanley–Stafford Beaconside route in 2003. One of the three, YJ54 CFA (No. 186) is seen here waiting time outside Stafford railway station before returning to Hanley on the X1 in November 2007.

Bakers operated four ex-Burnley & Pendle, but new to Stagecoach Manchester, Alexander ALX200-bodied Volvo B6BLEs. They all eventually received 'RU' cherished registrations such as 5777 RU (No. 217), seen at Biddulph under threatening skies in January 2009 before the Sainsbury's supermarket was built on the land behind it. It was formerly P244 JND.

Bakerbus 9595 RU (No. 194) was a Wright-bodied Scania L113 that was new to Orkney operator White of Bridge of Walls as N162 KPS. It later passed to Bob Smith Travel of Durham before arriving at Bakers and is seen laying over in Biddulph in 2006 after working a 94 from Newcastle.

In 2007 Bakers won a five-year Cheshire County Council contract to run the new coordinated 'Beartown Bus' local bus network in Congleton. Three brand new Plaxton Primo midibuses were delivered in a new two-tone green livery for the services. DX07 WEF 'Stardust' (No. 205) is seen laying over in Congleton Fairground bus station in May 2010.

Bakerbus Alexander Dash-bodied Volvo B6 L662 MSF (No. 227) looks very smart in Congleton as it waits to depart for Biddulph in April 2011. The bus was new to Stagecoach Fife Scottish and is an example of the then Stagecoach standard bus.

Following tender wins in 2008 Bakerbus ordered some Enviro 200s from Alexander Dennis to work routes 392 and 393 between Macclesfield to Stockport. Very occasionally these buses appeared on other routes in the Potteries, such as KX58 GSZ (No. 223) approaching Stoke station on a journey to Stone on the X1 in April 2011.

The most impressive buses ever operated by Bakers were three Wright Eclipse Gemini-bodied Volvo B5LH hybrid double-deckers new in October 2011 for the X1 service from Hanley to Stafford Beaconside. They also made appearances on the 9 from Hanley to Biddulph. DX61 EOP (No. 247) is seen at Fegg Hayes in July 2014 while working on the 9 back to Biddulph. Unfortunately these impressive vehicles only lasted three years at Bakers following the sale of the company to Island Fortitude and its subsequent demise.

The only other double-deckers in the Bakers fleet were four Dennis Tridents with Plaxton President bodywork, new to Metroline in 2003 as dual-door buses but later converted to single-door. LR52 KVO (No. 265) is seen at Smallthorne in July 2013 on its way to Biddulph. It was formerly Metroline TP 349.

Bakers went on to operate a large fleet of Optare Solos of various lengths and widths. MX54 KXY (No. 197) is seen at Congleton in April 2011 ready to work a 99 to Biddulph. This bus was new to Alton Towers Transport.

Bakers built up a small fleet of youthful early model Wright Streetlite WF single-deckers. MX60 BXC (No. 253) is seen at Newcastle-under-Lyme working an X75 to Keele in October 2012. All these Streetlites would later pass to D&G Bus in January 2015 along with the sale of the Bakers bus services.

Three ex-Menzies Aviation of Heathrow Airport Scania Omnicity single-deckers were acquired to increase capacity on the X1 Hanley–Stafford Beaconside service. They kept the silver livery but were lettered up to promote the X1 service. YS03 ZKX is seen reversing off the stand at the old Hanley bus station on its way to Stafford Beaconside on 20 September 2010.

Bassetts Coachways of Tittensor operated some bus services around the Stone and Stafford area using coaches. Plaxton Premiere 320-bodied Dennis Javelin M882 WFA, seen here in Hanley in November 1996, was new to the company in January 1995. Bassetts closed the coach business in 2003 to concentrate on its haulage business.

Possibly one of the rarest vehicles to run in the Potteries was A309 KDD, a Quest 80 with Locomotors bodywork operated by Bennetts of Cranberry in their original brown and buff livery. It is seen here in Shelton. It was new to the National Star Centre of Further Education.

Bennetts of Cranberry later changed their livery from brown and buff to purple, as seen by Plaxton Pointer-bodied Dennis Dart MPD T48 JBA at Newcastle working a Sunday tendered service on the 164 from Market Drayton in June 2015. This bus was purchased new by the company in 1999.

The Berresfords Motors fleet contained many interesting vehicles and is still sadly missed today. Park Royal-bodied AEC Reliance JPA 179K, seen here leaving Hanley for Leek in August 1984, was new to London Country Bus Services as Green Line coach RP 79 in 1972 and arrived at Berresfords in 1979 when only seven years old.

Another ex-London Country RP Class AEC Reliance to work for Berresfords was similar JPA 145K, but this one has received a replacement BET-style front as a result of accident damage. It is also seen leaving Hanley on 11 July 1982 working a 16 to Leek despite being lettered up for the X1 Derby–Manchester Derbyman service.

CFS 108L seen here at Berresfords Cheddleton garage was a twenty-five-seater ex-Lothian Buses Seddon Pennine. It would later pass on loan to Pooles Coachways, but never returned despite the deal to purchase Pooles never being completed. A similar vehicle CFS 109L worked for Stoniers.

In the early 1980s Berresfords hired three ex-Bournemouth Corporation Weyman-bodied Leyland Atlanteans and later went on to purchase them. They initially ran in Bournemouth yellow livery, but AEL 178B had received fleet livery when seen here at Cheddleton Garage on 16 May 1982.

Two Willowbrook-bodied Ford 192 service buses arrived at Berresfords from Highland Scottish in this grey livery in 1982 during the Falklands War and they subsequently gained the nickname 'troop buses' because of their austere look. KST 367G is seen here leaving Hanley in grey with a Berresfords sticker on 5 August 1982. They both later received fleet livery.

Willowbrook-bodied Ford 192 KST 360G looks smarter and not as austere after a repaint into Berresfords red and ivory livery. It is seen here when parked up outside sister company Stoniers' garage at Tunstall in January 1984.

LCM 160G was one of a pair of Northern Counties-bodied Leyland Atlanteans in the Berresfords fleet that were new to Birkenhead Corporation later passing to Merseyside PTE. It is seen here working for Stoniers and parked up at their Tunstall garage on 7 April 1985.

NWA 262K was one of four Daimler Fleetlines purchased by Berresfords in 1984. It was new to Sheffield Corporation but later passed to South Yorkshire PTE. Seen here parked up at Cheddleton garage on 8 July 1984, it was the only one of the four to receive Berresfords livery – the other three went to Stoniers.

Berresfords Alexander-bodied Daimler Fleetline NXA 623H looks very smart when seen at Bucknall working a Sunday morning 16 Hanley–Leek service on 20 October 1985. It was new to Fife Scottish and had only just recently been repainted into Berresfords livery.

The Berresford Group operated six of these Pennine-bodied AEC Swifts with a further two acquired for spares. They were new to Rochdale Corporation, later passing to Greater Manchester PTE. TDK 543K is in Berresfords livery but working for Stoniers when seen parked up at their Tunstall garage.

Berresfords operated a batch of these ex-North Western Road Car Willowbrook-bodied AEC Reliances. Those with bus seats received red fleet livery, but those with dual-purpose seating received ivory. VDB 951 looks immaculate in the all-over ivory livery outside Stoniers garage in Parsonage Street Tunstall on 16 May 1982.

Berresfords former City of Oxford Motor Services Willowbrook-bodied AEC Reliance SWL 49J leaves Hanley bus station with a 16 to Leek in May 1984. It was acquired with the business of Smiths of Waterhouses.

Other AEC Swifts operated by Berresfords were two Marshall-bodied examples that were new to St Helens Corporation and later passing to Merseyside PTE. One was PDJ 277L, seen here ready to leave Cheddleton garage for Leek.

Berresfords MCW-bodied Leyland Atlantean LAK 289G carries a healthy load as it reverses off the stand at the old Hanley bus station working a 16 to Leek. This was a joint service with Procters and PMT. The bus was new to Bradford Corporation in 1968, later passing to West Yorkshire PTE.

One of the last vehicles to enter service with Berresfords before the sale to PMT in April 1987 was PCH 418L, an ex-Trent Bristol RELH with ECW coach bodywork seen here in Stafford Street, Hanley. Following the sale to PMT, this bus would later become the only Berresfords or Stoniers vehicle to receive the PMT red and yellow fleet livery.

Blink and you missed this one! Best Bus started operating commercially between Crewe and Nantwich in January 2008, replacing the subsidised Arriva services 44 and 45 between the two towns. It only lasted four months before collapsing in May 2008. Former Chester Reeve Burgess Pointer Dennis Dart J53 EDM is seen leaving Crewe on a 44 for Nantwich.

Boydons of Winkhill operated rural route 451 between Winkhill and Leek using this unusual Wright-bodied Leyland Cub JXI 6133. It is seen resting between duties at Leek bus station.

Choice Travel of Wednesfield was purchased by D&G Bus in 2006 and its vehicles eventually went on to carry the blue and cream livery. Plaxton Pointer-bodied Dennis Dart OUI 9143 (No. 103) is seen at Stafford working an 880 to Codsall in June 2009. The bus was new to Petes Travel West Bromwich as T428 EBD.

Copelands of Meir used two ex-PMT Reeve Burgess-bodied Dennis Darts on its only bus service 40 between Longton and Fenton via Hollybush Estate and Heron Cross. MIB 783, seen here on the Hollybush Estate, was new to PMT in 1992 as J914 SEH.

Copelands ran this former London Country North West Duple Dartline-bodied Dennis Dart H243 MUK for a while, but it never received fleet livery. It is seen at Fenton working a 40 back to Longton.

The two older ex-PMT high-floor Dennis Darts were later replaced with low-floor Plaxton Pointer-bodied Dennis Dart SLF models such as MIB 797, seen here in Longton bus station looking immaculate as usual for Copelands vehicles.

A second low-floor Plaxton Pointer-bodied Dennis Dart SLF was acquired from the auction of the assets of Procters of Fenton following its collapse in March 2013. MIB 302 wore an adapted version of both Copelands and Procters livery and is seen here at Fenton. It was new to Trent as S942 UAL.

Plaxton Pointer-bodied Dennis Dart JJZ 5248 (No. 112) wears a modified D&G livery with more blue when seen at Sneyd Green. It was new to Bleasdale Liverpool as DE51 EWJ.

D&G Bus took delivery of the first three Stoke-on-Trent City Council-owned Alexander-bodied Dennis Darts in their attractive Cityrider livery in February 2002. DA51 XTE (No. 31) is seen when brand new parked opposite the original D&G Bus garage in Longton before entering service the following day.

D&G Bus Wright Handybus-bodied Dennis Dart K856 PCN (No. 17) is seen reversing off the stand at the old Hanley bus station. It was new to Wear Buses Sunderland. D&G Bus operated Dennis Darts with bodywork from a variety of different manufacturers.

Alexander ALX200-bodied Dennis Dart YD02 RGY is seen at Chesterton after just being painted into D&G Bus blue and cream livery at the local Reliance Bus Works, shortly after being acquired from Quantock Motor Services of Bishops Lydeard.

Wright Cadet-bodied DAF SB120 YN03 PMX (No. 125) is seen at Congleton working Cheshire County Council contracted service 42 to Crewe via Holmes Chapel in the new two-tone red D&G Bus livery. It was one of four similar buses acquired from Strawberry Buses of St Helens, but was new to Dublin Bus.

A unique bus in the D&G Bus fleet was Optare Tempo MX06 ADV (No. 18), seen here at Adderley Green depot after being repainted into this stunning two-tone green livery for the Buxton Flyer service 118 Hanley–Buxton. It was new to Alton Towers Transport so had previously worked in the Stoke-on-Trent area.

Following the purchase of Wardle Transport from Arriva in May 2015 some former Arriva London buses joined the fleet such as Plaxton Pointer-bodied Dennis Dart X546 GGO (No. 185) seen at Chell Heath working a 9 to Hanley in February 2016.

Three double-deckers were also acquired with the purchase of Wardle Transport from Arriva, and they too were ex-Arriva London examples. Alexander ALX 400-bodied DAF 250 X441 FGP (No. 179) is seen at Westwood School Leek before working back to Hanley in June 2015.

Before the sale of South Lancs Travel to Diamond in early 2015, four recently purchased brand new Alexander Dennis Enviro 200s were transferred to the D&G Bus fleet and initially worked in South Lancs Travel blue white and yellow livery with D&G fleetnames. SL64 JGV (No. 33) is seen at Penkhull working former RML Travel route 41 to Birches Head in May 2015.

Two MCV Evolution-bodied DAF 180s were purchased new by D&G-owned Midland of Wednesfield for use at Walsall, but were later transferred back to D&G at Crewe before the sale of Midland to Arriva. YJ60 GGV (No. 133) is seen at Congleton shortly afterwards in March 2015.

Two Dennis Darts with East Lancs Mylennium bodywork were included in the five buses acquired with the bus services of Routemaster Buses of Crewe in 2016. PL05 PLO (No. 163) has received a repaint into D&G red when seen here at Heron Cross on former Copelands route 40 to Fenton in July 2016. It was new to Epsom Buses Quality Line.

D&G Bus Plaxton Pointer-bodied Dennis Dart T467 HNH (No. 187) was painted into a Tesco all-over advertisement for the free service to the Tesco supermarket at Crewe. It is seen here at Adderley Green Garage in April 2016. The bus was new to Pete's Travel West Bromwich.

Wright Streetlite WF MX60 GXC (No. 154) was one of seven similar buses acquired with the bus services of Bakerbus Biddulph in January 2015. It had received a repaint into D&G red when seen at Congleton in August 2016.

D&G Bus still operates four Stoke-on-Trent City Council-owned Optare Versas on various contracted routes in the city but they occasionally stray onto other D&G routes, such as WT58 BUS (No. 171) at Chell Heath working a 9 to Hanley in July 2015.

Two Wright Commander-bodied DAF 220s were also acquired with the Routemaster Buses business in 2016. They had been new to Fishwicks of Leyland. YJ53 VDT (No. 148) is seen here at Meir Square after a repaint into D&G livery in April 2019.

D&G Bus acquired six Optare Versas from Bournemouth Yellow buses in 2018 and all bar one were repainted red. Surprisingly they kept their select registrations. T20 TYB (No. 20) is seen at Congleton bus station working a 94 to Newcastle in September 2021. This bus was withdrawn shortly afterwards after receiving accident damage.

D&G Bus operated three ex-Nottingham Scania Omnicity single-deckers on its trunk route 85 between Hanley and Crewe via Newcastle. YN04 GMV (No. 6041) is seen at Shelton approaching Stoke railway station in September 2012. These buses were later transferred to South Lancs Travel.

Certain buses in the D&G Bus fleet are in different colours for different routes. Optare Versa YJ57 XWB (No. 158) is one of six buses in the fleet that wears the 'Yellow 9' livery for the Biddulph–Clayton route seen here at Westbury Park in June 2021. The bus was new to Transdev Burnley & Pendle.

Seven buses wear this orange livery for routes 1 and 1A from Meir to Silverdale and Wood Lane. Ex-Hatts of Salisbury Alexander Dennis Enviro 200 SN11 FFU (No. 111) is seen arriving at Longton bus station in September 2015 and is one of four Enviro 200s and three Optare Solos to wear this livery.

Four Alexander Dennis Enviro 200s were painted two-tone blue for the 'Blue 2' from Birches Head to Westbury Park, such as YX09 FML (No. 41) seen at Westbury Park in May 2018. Route 2 was later altered to only run between Hanley and Birches Head so only required one bus. This bus was also new to First London.

Two of the Alexander Dennis Enviro 200s that originally carried Blue 2 livery now wear this attractive brown and cream livery for the 8A and 8B Hanley–Brown Edge–Endon routes that were once operated by Turner's of Brown Edge before its sale to PMT in 1987. D&G Bus took over these routes after PMT discontinued running them. YX09 FME (No. 38) is seen waiting time at the Robin Hood Norton in August 2021.

To celebrate the twentieth anniversary of D&G Bus in 2018, Plaxton Pointer-bodied Dennis Dart CHZ 8960 (No. 10) was repainted into the original blue and cream livery and regained its former fleet number, 10. This was the first new bus to be purchased by D&G in 2004 as DK54 KKY. It is seen in Congleton in May 2019.

D&G Bus purchased the Cannock operations of Arriva Midlands in January 2020, and with it a number of buses. These initially ran in Arriva livery with Chaserider stickers such as Wright Commander-bodied DAF SB220 FJ06 ZTL (No. 188) seen here at Stafford in April 2021.

Some vehicles acquired with the Cannock operations of Arriva Midlands carried the latest Arriva pale blue livery. One such vehicle was Plaxton Pointer-bodied Dennis Dart SLF FJ54 OTT (No. 8), seen here at Stafford in April 2021.

GHA Coaches of Ruabon won Cheshire East Council tenders to operate services in the Crewe and Congleton areas, even reaching into Kidsgrove on the 77 from Congleton. Former London United Marshall-bodied Dennis Dart T112 KGP is seen at Congleton in March 2015.

Two brand new Alexander Dennis Enviro 200 buses were purchased by GHA in 2015 to work the Congleton 'Beartown Bus' town service. They carried an attractive lime green livery featuring bears. YY15 CMZ (No. 1472) is seen in Congleton bus station in April 2015 heading for the Bromley Estate on a 90.

GHA also purchased three brand new Enviro 200s for service 42 from Congleton to Crewe via Holmes Chapel. These carried GHA Gold branding. They only lasted just over a year on this route as GHA went into receivership in July 2016. YY15 CNC (No. 1406) is seen waiting time in Congleton in April 2015 when brand new.

Matthews Motors/Handybus mainly operated a fleet of elderly minibuses of various makes, but there were a couple of interesting larger vehicles present in the fleet. One such vehicle was ex-Eastern Scottish Alexander-bodied Seddon Pennine 7 ESC 844S seen here at Ball Green.

Handybus also ran two ECW-bodied Bristol LH service buses. One was TPJ 56S, a short Bristol LHS that was new to London Country Bus Services. It is seen here in Silverdale working from Park Site to Newcastle on a route formerly worked by Pooles Coachways.

Following the collapse of GHA Coaches in 2016, Cheshire East Council retendered the Congleton Beartown Bus network and local coach operator Hollinsheads of Biddulph won the five year contract and purchased two Alexander Dennis Enviro 200s to work it. SN66 WKZ is seen at Congleton in plain white livery in August 2021.

Knotty Bus and Coach operated a fascinating fleet of elderly vehicles from a bygone era on local service work around Stoke-on-Trent in the early 1990s. CYA 181J was a Plaxon Derwent-bodied AEC Reliance new to Hutchins and Cornelius of South Petherton and is seen here on the Norton Estate heading back to Hanley.

AEC Swifts operating on local bus services in the 1990s were very rare indeed, but Knotty Bus ran a handful of them – including ex-St Helens and Merseyside PTE GEM 598N, a Marshall-bodied dual-door example seen here leaving the Chatterley Whitfield mining museum at Chell.

A second former St Helens Marshall-bodied dual-door AEC Swift to enter service with Knotty Bus was EDJ 242J. It has yet to receive a destination blind when seen here at Chell Heath.

Looking very smart in Knotty Bus black, white and grey livery at Chell Heath is JPA 171K, an AEC Reliance with Park Royal bodywork that was new to London Country Bus Services as Green Line coach RP 71 in 1972.

Another AEC Swift in the Knotty Bus fleet was Alexander-bodied JPF 103K. This was also new to London Country as Green Line coach SMA 3 and is seen here at Bradwell on its way to Chesterton.

Knotty Bus OFR 983M was a former Blackpool Transport Marshall-bodied AEC Swift, seen here in Burslem in 1993 carrying an advert celebrating five years of Knotty Buses.

Another ex-Blackpool Transport vehicle in the Knotty Bus fleet was this Marshall Camair-bodied Dennis Lancet VCY 598Y, seen here at Stone working a 252 back to Longton in 1994.

Ladyline Coaches of Key Green Congleton ran this Duple Dominant bus-bodied Bedford YMQ FBX 562W on local services in the town. It is seen at the Fairground bus station in the original cream livery. The bus was new to Davies of Camarthen.

Ladyline also operated some double-deckers for school work, but these occasionally ventured onto service work, such as Roe-bodied Leyland Atlantean AUP 369N here at Congleton Fairground working a 92 to Buglawton Estate. This bus was new to Northern General.

Ladyline also operated an ex-London Transport Bristol LH, OJD 55R. It is seen in the original Ladyline cream livery at Congleton Fairground bus station working to West Heath. It was formerly London Transport BL 55.

OJD 55R is shown again in this photo, but has now received a coat of orange paint and the Ladyline Local fleetname when see at Rode Heath. It came to Ladyline from OK Motor Services Bishop Auckland.

Ladyline had a varied fleet containing many different vehicles at different times, such as this Reeve Burgess-bodied Leyland Swift G142 TBD, seen here at Congleton working to Buglawton Estate. It was new as an unregistered Leyland development vehicle and was purchased and registered by MK Citybus in 1999.

A long lasting double-decker in the Ladyline fleet that has only just been replaced was this ex-London Transport Leyland Titan B113 WUV. It later transferred from Stagecoach Selkent in London to Stagecoach Tansit, where it was converted to single-door and had a three-track number blind fitted. It is seen at Congleton Fairground in June 2016.

The latest double-decker in the Ladyline fleet is Alexander ALX400-bodied Volvo B7L X931 YCC, seen at Congleton in June 2022. It was new to Dublin Bus as 00-D-40029 and carries the latest lime green livery. The blind still shows a destination from previous owner, Tyrers.

Midland Classic of Burton started running into Uttoxeter after purchasing the Burton operations from Arriva Midlands in 2016. Alexander Dennis Enviro 400 SN11 BMU (No. 63) was painted into the former Burton-on-Trent Corporation livery and is seen here in Uttoxeter in July 2019 working the 406 outer circle service. Ironically Burton Corporation buses never ran into Uttoxeter!

Some rather unique buses to operate in the Midland Classic of Burton fleet is a batch of Scania Irizar i3 buses, such as YN17 ONJ (No. 17) – seen here in Uttoxeter in September 2021 working the 406 Outer Circle service. This bus was new to Reading Buses.

A brand new bus to arrive at Midland Classic in 2021 was DV21 OPM (No. 10), a Volvo B8RLE with MCV EvoRa bodywork seen here leaving Uttoxeter with a 403 to Burton-on-Trent in September 2021.

Most of the bus services acquired from Arriva Midlands with the Burton depot in 2016 were originally operated by Stevensons of Spath. Stevensons had themselves been purchased by British Bus in 1994. Wright Solar-bodied Scania L94 TFA 13 (No. 75) wears a heritage Stevensons livery when seen in Uttoxeter on the 406 Outer Circle, a former Stevensons route, in June 2022. The bus was formerly YN04 ANX.

Moorland Buses based at Weston Coyney operated a fleet of minibuses in this attractive blue and cream livery between Meir Square and Newcastle via Longton and Stoke. Freight Rover Sherpa E135 RAX is seen at Newcastle in July 2003.

Nova Scotia Travel of Middlewich ran into Hanley for a short time on the Staffordshire County Council contracted service X70 from Winsford. Leyland National GNV 659N is seen leaving Hanley bus station for Winsford. It was new to United Counties. Nova Scotia Travel also operated the Alsager town service for a while too.

Paragon Travel of Uttoxeter was a short-lived operator that ran the 428 service between Uttoxeter and Lichfield. Berkhof-bodied Dennis Lance M197 UAN is seen outside the former Stevensons garage at Spath in June 2010. The bus still carries a destination blind from its time at Avon Buses on the Wirral, but was new as an airport bus at Heathrow Airport.

Another visitor to the area that was based outside it was Pete's Travel of West Bromwich, West Midlands. It ran into Hanley on the council-tendered service 351 from Telford. Wright Handybus-bodied Dnnis Dart K571 PDY is seen at Newcastle-under-Lyme.

Pooles Coachways of Alsagers Bank was an old established independent operator serving the Newcastle-under-Lyme area. Most of its vehicles were purchased new, but Pennine-bodied Leyland Leopard NTD 117K (No. 3), seen in the Ironmarket, Newcastle, was new to Lancaster City Council.

Pooles Coachways built up a fleet of BET style Willowbrook-bodied Leyland Leopard service buses such as NRE 582L (No5) in the smart ivory and red livery, seen here in Newcastle bus station. The bus was purchased new to the company in 1973.

Similar Willowbrook-bodied Leyland Leopard RBF 987M (No. 7) is seen picking up a passenger in Ironmarket, Newcastle. This bus was later rebodied with a Willowbrook Warrior body by Maynes of Manchester.

The final Willowbrook-bodied Leyland Leopard purchased new by Pooles was LBF 796P, seen here laying over in Newcastle bus station in winter covered in a liberal coating of grime.

The final vehicle purchased new by Pooles Coachways was another Leyland Leopard, but due to capacity problems at the usual bodybuilders Willowbrook, it was-bodied by Marshalls of Cambridge with their unusual Camair bodywork. XFA 967S (No. 9) is seen here in Ironmarket, Newcastle, on 1 August 1985.

Pooles Coachways also ran this Park Royal-bodied AEC Reliance JPA 120K, seen here on a dull winter day in Newcastle. It was owned by Berresfords Motors and was loaned during the period that Berresfords was negotiating to purchase the Pooles business. The deal was never signed so Pooles remained independent, but the bus never returned.

Another loan vehicle from Berresfords was Seddon Pennine CFS 108L. This also never returned to Berresfords and later passed to hauliers G&B McCready, who subsequently purchased Pooles. A new two-tone blue and white livery was introduced along with the Pooles Travel fleetname. The new image didn't last long as shortly afterwards the Pooles services were sold to PMT.

Following the sale of Pooles Coachways to McCreadys, this Leyland National GUG 118N was acquired and repainted into the new two-tone blue and white livery with Pooles Travel fleetnames. It is seen here laying over in Newcastle bus station.

Procters of Hanley was another of the well-established Potteries independent bus operator running double-deckers into Hanley on its service 16 to Leek. Alexander-bodied Daimler Fleetline AVT 249C was new to the company in 1965 and is seen at the garage in the old blue and cream livery on 7 May 1981.

A youthful purchase by Procters in 1981 was this four-year-old ex-Tayside Regional Council Alexander-bodied dual-door Bristol VRLL, OSR 204R. It is seen parked up at the old Hanley bus station on 27 September 1982 in full Tayside livery but with Procters fleetnames applied. Procters kept this bus in Tayside livery and later adopted this for the other double-deckers in the fleet.

Procters purchased two Leyland Atlanteans in 1974 with Alexander AL bodywork identical to those being delivered at the time to Greater Glasgow PTE with panoramic windows. These were the last new double-deckers to be purchased by Procters. GBF 279N is seen arriving into Hanley from Leek. It has received a modified front panel due to accident damage.

The other Alexander AL-bodied Leyland Atlantean in the Procters fleet was GBF 278N. It is seen laying over in Leek bus station shortly after deregulation in 1986, bearing the Staffordshire Bus logo indicating a journey subsidised by the council.

Following a period using grant coaches on route 16 Procters later added Plaxton Pointer-bodied Dennis Darts and a Volvo B6R to their fleet, such as ex-Busways Travel Dennis Dart L754 VNL seen here at the Fenton garage in the new white, blue and orange livery.

The very last bus purchased by Procters was its only low-floor vehicle. Plaxton Pointer-bodied Dennis Dart SLF TLZ 9469 is seen leaving Hanley bus station for Leek in July 2011. It was new as S942 UAL to Trent Buses. It would last barely two years in service before the company suddenly collapsed in March 2013.

RML Travel started operations in 2006 with route 40 between Hanley and Birches Head in competition with First Potteries. Its first bus was RIB 7002 (DZZ 1), a Dennis Dart with the unique one-off Zig-Zag bodywork, which was a reworked Carlyle Dartline body. It is seen here at Diana Road Birches Head.

Occasionally RML Travel would put its Routemaster out on service 40 CUV 327C (RML 2327). It is seen here on the Birches Head Estate displaying a full set of London-style blinds. Despite appearances it was new as a green-liveried London Transport Country area bus in 1965.

RML Travel later ran a handful of ex-Trent Buses Optare Metroriders including N206 VRC (MRL 206), seen here at Longton with blinds set for route 64 to Market Drayton.

An unusual vehicle to operate in the RML Travel fleet was former PMT Ami-bodied Mercedes Benz 811D G330 XRE (MA 330), in competition against PMT on the Hanley to Birches Head route. It is seen here in Birches Head with temporary blinds.

An early Optare Metrorider operated by RML Travel was J555 RML seen here at Birches Head. It was new to London Buses as J210 BWU. It regained its former London Buses fleet number MRL 210 with RML Travel.

RML Travel also ran this Alexander Dash-bodied Volvo B6R M746 PRS. It is seen here on the extended route 41 to Clayton. This bus was new to Stagecoach and spent some time on loan to Greater Manchester Buses South when it was still an employee-owned company.

RML Travel also operated this rebodied Leyland Tiger that had its original Duple Dominant coach body replaced by an East Lancs bus body. YDZ 3458 (TEL 458) is seen at Birches Head. It was new to National Welsh as A226 VWO.

Routemaster Buses of Crewe ran into Hanley and Newcastle on the Fridays-only route 79 to Nantwich. An unusual vehicle working the service is Alexander-bodied Volvo Olympian G706 TCD (No. L706), seen here at Newcastle in June 2016. It was new to Southdown.

Routemaster Buses ran this ex-Bournemouth Yellow Buses East Lancs-bodied Dennis Dart N466 TPK (No. DT466). It is seen laying over in Hinde Street, Hanley, in July 2016 in Routemaster Buses' smart two-tone green livery.

Routemaster Buses PL05 PLN (No. SD38) was one of three ex-Epsom Buses Quality Line East Lancs Mylennium-bodied Dennis Darts in the fleet. It is seen here in Newcastle-under-Lyme in April 2016 working to Nantwich. These buses also worked tendered routes in Crewe.

Another Dennis Dart in the Routemaster Buses fleet was Alexander ALX 200-bodied X616 JCS (No. SLD616), seen laying over at Hanley's Hinde Street in May 2016. It was new to Stagecoach Western Scottish.

The only double-decker ever operated by Scraggs of Bucknall was 6879 VT a Volvo Olympian with Alexander bodywork seen here at Bentilee in the smart two-tone brown Scraggs livery. It was new to Stagecoach Fife Scottish as K710 ASC.

Scraggs operated a handful of Optare Solos on various council-tendered services. 1580 VT is seen here at Stanfields working a 90 from Tunstall to Ball Green in the Blue Buses livery in March 2016. This bus was new to Stoke-on-Trent City Council for its Cityrider fleet as YJ05 JXR, but later purchased by Scraggs.

Scraggs once operated a small fleet of Plaxton Primo midibuses such as 5437 VT, seen looking very smart here at Abbey Hulton in May 2011 in the Blue Buses livery. This bus was new to Trustybus Hertfordshire as MK55 WDA.

Select Bus Services runs a varied fleet in south of the area in an attractive dark red livery. Wright Commander-bodied DAF SB220 FJ06 ZTH (No. 25), seen here in Stafford in April 2021, was new to Arriva, passing to D&G Bus with the sale of the Cannock depot in January 2021. It subsequently moved on to Select.

Select Bus Services runs into Stone on the 103 from Eccleshall. Plaxton Pointer-bodied Dennis Dart SLF GX06 DXA (No. 22) is seen at Stone after arriving from Eccleshall. The bus was new to Stagecoach South.

Stantons of Stoke ran two ex-Wardle Transport Alexander ALX400-bodied Dennis Tridents such as 815 DYE, seen here at Northwood in May 2015 in the original Stantons livery. It was new to Stagecoach London as T698 KPU.

Stantons of Stoke run a small fleet of Optare Solos on services around Stoke-on-Trent. BU54 ALL is seen here on the Norton Estate working from Ball Green to Tunstall in September 2018. This bus was new to Stoke-on-Trent City Council for its Cityrider fleet and was subsequently purchased by Stantons.

Stantons of Stoke also have some Alexander Dennis Enviro 200s in its fleet, such as 8710 VT – seen leaving Bradeley in June 2021. It was new to Bus Eireann in 2009 as 09-D-3731.

New additions to the Stantons of Stoke fleet in 2022 were a pair of ex-Lothian Buses Wright Gemini-bodied B9TL double-deckers used mainly for schools and Stoke City FC football shuttles, but occasionally used on service work such as LRV 731 at Pinfold Avenue, Norton, working a 90 from Ball Green to Tunstall shortly after being repainted into fleet livery. It was new as SN09 CUG.

Stanways of Rode Heath run a varied fleet on contract and service work. The first brand new bus purchased was Optare Solo DX07 WFA in August 2007, used for Cheshire East Council contracted service 315 from Congleton to Rode Heath with morning and evening trips on the 321 to Newcastle. It is seen here at Congleton Fairground.

Stanways ran this rare Alexander P type-bodied Leyland Tiger E930 PBE seen here at Congleton Fairground bus station working a school service in October 2015. It was new to Grimsby Cleethorpes Transport.

Route 90, the Kidsgrove Town Service, was run by Stanways on contract to Staffordshire County Council. The regular bus for this service was Plaxton Pointer-bodied Dennis Dart MPD JIG 8878 seen here climbing up Stonebank Road Kidsgrove in June 2016. It was new to Go North East as X513 WRG.

Stanways also ran this Alexander Dash-bodied Dennis Dart P450 KRP, seen at Congleton Fairground standing in for the usual Optare Solo on the 315 to Rode Heath in April 2012. It was new to Stagecoach United Counties.

Stevensons of Spath was an old established independent operator based in Uttoxeter that became more prominent in the Potteries area after purchasing Crystal Coaches of Newcastle in September 1984. East Lancs-bodied Leyland Titan PD3 82 HBC (No. 54) is seen in Newcastle shortly afterwards in November 1984. New to Leicester Corporation, it was reregistered RRF 109B in February 1985.

Stevensons ran a handful of half-cab double-deckers well into the 1980s and was the last operator of such buses in the Potteries. PCW 946 (No. 29) was a Northern Counties-bodied Leyland Titan PD2 new to Burnley Colne and Nelson and is seen parked at the former Crystal Coaches depot at Newcastle in the snow in February 1985.

Stevensons was one of the first independents to run a Routemaster in service. This, however, was not an ex-London Transport example but was ex-Northern General RCN 699 (No. 52), a Park Royal-bodied front entrance example seen here at Spath Garage Uttoxeter on 1 March 1982 alongside brand new Bristol VRT UVT 49X.

Stevensons FHG 158E (No. 30) was a Leyland Titan PD2 with East Lancs bodywork new to Burnley Colne and Nelson in 1967. It is seen on the fuelling pump a Spath garage in the low winter sun on 3 March 1982.

Massey-bodied Leyland Titan PD3 PAX 466F (No. 30) was new to Bedwas & Machen in 1968 and carried the last traditional sunken gangway low-bridge body built. It came to Stevensons in November 1982 and is seen at Spath garage.

Stevensons JKE 335E (No. 38) was a Leyland Atlantean PDR1 with boxy Massey bodywork. It was new to Maidstone Borough Council and is seen at Spath on the fuelling point on 3 March 1982.

Stevensons of Uttoxeter operated forty-five ex-London Transport DMS class Daimler Fleetlines and purchased many more for spares. One such was Park Royal-bodied JGF 241K (No. 37), former DMS 241, seen here in Newcastle on a former Crystal Coaches working on 1 April 1985.

Stevensons purchased a pair of youthful Leyland Olympians with East Lancs bodies from Eastbourne Corporation in January 1983. B101 PHC (No. 91) is seen parked next to sister B102 PHC (No. 92) at Spath garage.

Stevensons operated this former Rhymney Valley East Lancs-bodied Leyland Leopard DUH 77V (No. 102). It has received a new plain front panel when seen here at the Burslem garage that had replaced the former Crystal Coaches depot at Newcastle.

Stevensons operated eight of these former South Yorkshire PTE Optare-bodied Dennis Dominos such as C47 HDT (No. 229) seen parked at the Burslem garage between duties.

East Lancs-bodied Bristol RE HTD 342K (No. 67), seen here in Uttoxeter, came into the Stevensons fleet following the merger with East Staffordshire District Council. It had been new to Darwin Corporation.

Stevensons of Spath only ever operated one ex-London Transport ECW-bodied Bristol LH. OJD 89R (No. 24) is seen on the fuel pump at Spath garage on 3 March 1982. It was former London Transport BL89.

Stevensons went on to operate many Dennis Darts with bodywork from various different bodybuilders. An early example is Duple Dartline-bodied G141 GOL (No. 41), seen at Chatterley Whitfield Mining Museum. It was new as a Dennis demonstrator.

HXI 3011 (No. 261) was one of a few Leyland Lynx not to receive the standard Leyland bodywork. Instead it received Alexander Belfast N type bodywork and was new to Citybus Belfast in 1992. It is seen here at Spath garage after joining the Stevensons fleet. Stevensons ran seven of these buses, the only examples to run outside Northern Ireland.

Stevensons purchased four of these youthful Alexander RH-bodied Metrobuses that had been prematurely withdrawn by West Yorkshire PTE before the formation of Yorkshire Rider at deregulation. UWW 517X (No. 76) is seen on the fuel pump at Spath shortly after arriving at Stevensons in May 1987.

A unique vehicle in the Stevensons fleet was ECW-bodied Leyland Olympian B45 prototype Q246 FVT (No. 99). It arrived as an unregistered shell devoid of any seating having been used by Leyland as a test vehicle. It was fitted out by Stevensons with seats from DMS Daimler Fleetlines. It is seen here at Spath on the fuel pump.

Stevensons purchased two coach-seated National Bus Company standard ECW-bodied Bristol VRTs new and operated a handful of second-hand examples too. UVT 49X (No. 49) was new in October 1981 and was the final Bristol VRT chassis to be produced, but not the last to be bodied. It is seen here on a private hire at Blackpool in 1986.

West Yorkshire PTE disposed of many youthful buses shortly before deregulation as Yorkshire Rider didn't want to take over their expensive leases. Stevensons snapped up some of these, such as Roe-bodied Leyland Olympian UWW 6X (No. 95), seen here at Spath in May 1987. It didn't last very long in the fleet, being withdrawn by early 1991.

Stoniers of Goldenhill was a well established independent bus and coach operator that had been owned by Berresfords Motors since 1976 and ran a varied fleet double- and single-deckers around the Potteries. AEL 172B was one of a trio of MCW-bodied Leyland Atlanteans that were hired from Bournemouth Corporation and later purchased. It was the only one to receive Stoniers livery and is seen in Hanley on 8 June 1982.

Two four-year-old Northern Counties-bodied Leyland AN68 Atlanteans arrived at Stoniers in 1977 from Maidstone Corporation, where they were being replaced by Bedford single-deckers. They were the first rear-engined double-deckers in the Stoniers fleet. EKR 153L is seen passing through Town Road, Hanley, before it was pedestrianised on 3 August 1982.

Stoniers only ever operated two Leyland Nationals: a dual-door former Plymouth Corporation example (SCO 427L) and this former Hutchison of Overtown example (KVA 563L). This one was the first Leyland National to work in Scotland but was sold to Stoniers after a period with Irvines of Law. It is seen at the old garage at Goldenhill. A seized engine would lead to the premature withdrawl of both of them.

The first of three ex-London Country Park Royal-bodied AEC Reliances to join the Stoniers fleet was JPA 176K, formerly Green Line coach RP76. It is seen here parked up at the old Stoniers garage at Goldenhill on 7 December 1981. Two similar vehicles also entered service in the Berresfords Motors fleet.

LAK 296G was a MCW-bodied Leyland Atlantean PDR1/2 new to Bradford Corporation in 1968 and latterly working for West Yorkshire PTE. It was one of the last buses to be painted in this livery for Stoniers before the new 'more cream' livery was introduced. It is seen at the old Hanley bus station on 3 July 1983.

TDK 541J was one of a batch of six of these Pennine-bodied AEC Swifts that were new to Rochdale Corporation, later passing to Greater Manchester PTE. Stoniers and Berresfords had three each of these buses. It is seen parked at the old Goldenhill garage on 6 December 1981. It was the only one to have a 'J' registration. The other five had 'K' registrations.

FWJ 356J, seen here parked at Stoniers' Tunstall garage, was an Alexander-bodied Leyland Leopard that had been new to Sheffield, subsequently passing to South Yorkshire PTE. The Royal Doulton Churchbank pottery in the background is now a housing estate.

Stoniers operated this Alexander Y type Ford R1114 CST 707N, seen here looking very smart having just been repainted into fleet livery at Rothesthorpe services on the M1 while on its way to Showbus on 2 September 1984. It was formerly Highland Scottish T79.

The second ex-London Country Bus Services Park Royal-bodied AEC Reliance to join the Stoniers of Goldenhill fleet was JPA 181K. It was formerly Green Line coach RP81 and is seen at the Tunstall garage shortly after arrival on 16 May 1982.

Another photograph of the same ex-London Country Park Royal-bodied AEC Reliance JPA 181K showing how different it looks after receiving a BET-style front end following a collision with a skip lorry. It is seen parked up at the old Hanley bus station.

Stoniers ran two Seddon Pennine midibuses. XVU 334M was new to Greater Manchester PTE for use on the Centreline service linking Piccadilly and Victoria stations. In more rural surroundings it is seen in the snow at Mow Cop on 7 January 1985 working a 7 back to Tunstall.

The other Seddon Pennine midibus in the Stoniers fleet was CFS 109L, a former Lothian Regional Transport example. This differed from the ex-GMPTE example by having manual transmission. It is seen parked at the Tunstall garage.

The other ex-Bradford Corporation Alexander-bodied Leyland PDR1/2 Atlantean to run in the Stoniers fleet was LAK 292G. This bus is seen leaving the old Hanley bus station on 17 April 1984 in the new recently introduced 'more cream' Stoniers livery. Berresfords also ran LAK 289G, a similar vehicle in the same livery .

One of the last double-deckers to join the Stoniers fleet before the sale to PMT in 1987 was NXA 621H, an Alexander-bodied Daimler Fleetline that had been new to Highland Scottish. Another vehicle from the same batch joined the Berresfords fleet at the same time. It is seen at the old Hanley bus station in May 1985.

The third and final ex-London Country Park Royal-bodied AEC Reliance to join the Stoniers fleet was JPA 115K. It arrived a few years after the other examples in the fleet via Heart of England Tours and is seen leaving Hanley for Meir after being repainted into the latest Stoniers livery.

Another former South Yorkshire PTE vehicle to enter the Stoniers fleet was WET 176L, a Plaxton Derwent-bodied Seddon RU seen here parked up at the Tunstall garage in September 1983. It had been new to Rotherham Corporation.

NWA 263K, seen here in Burslem in August 1984, was one of three ex-South Yorkshire PTE Alexander AL-bodied Daimler Fleetlines to work in the Stoniers fleet. A fourth entered the Berresfords fleet. They were new to Sheffield Corporation in 1972.

Another Daimler Fleetline to join the Stoniers fleet was this Eastern Coach Works-bodied example, TGM 205J, new to Central Scottish and seen here in the old Hanley bus station on 28 April 1984. Its career with Stoniers ended prematurely when it was deroofed at the infamous Glebe Street bridge in Stoke.

One of the last single-deckers to join the Stoniers fleet before the sale to PMT was NPT 992M, a Plaxton Derwent-bodied AEC Reliance that was one of a pair new to Gillett Brothers, Quarrington Hill, Co. Durham, but came to Stoniers via Bickers of Coddenham, Suffolk. It ran for a while with Stoniers in Bickers green livery before being repainted.

Stoniers Pennine-bodied AEC Swift TDK 546K was the only one to receive a repaint into the new Stoniers livery complete with new style fleetnames, seen here leaving Hanley bus station for Eaton Park.

GYJ 404G was one of a pair of Alexander-bodied Daimler Fleetlines in the Stoniers fleet that had been new to Dundee Corporation later passing onto Tayside Regional Council. It is seen here in Kidsgrove on 6 January 1986 still in previous owner McLennans of Spittalfield's blue livery. It was never repainted into Stoniers livery.

Turner's of Brown Edge operated an immaculate fleet of double-deckers in a smart Tudor maroon and cream livery on its Hanley–Brown Edge service. Northern Counties-bodied Daimler Fleetline JBF 169N (No. 10) is seen passing through Market Square in Hanley before it was pedestrianised. This bus was new to the company in March 1975 and is now preserved.

Turner's Leyland Fleetline AFA 489S (No. 9) is seen leaving the old Hanley bus station for Brown Edge on 3 July 1982. It carries the latest more modern Northern Counties low-height bodywork with a curved windscreen and was the penultimate new double-decker to be purchased by Turner's in July 1978.

Northern Counties-bodied low-height Leyland Fleetline LVT 699V (No. 8) was the last new double-decker bus purchased by Turner's in April 1980. It is seen at Sneyd Green on its way from Brown Edge to Hanley in June 1982. This bus is now also preserved.

Up until 1982 Turner's had purchased all eight rear-engined double-deckers brand new. In following the end of Fleetline production decided to try two second-hand ex-London Transport Park Royal-bodied Daimler Fleetlines. The first one was OJD 128R (No. 5), seen here leaving Hanley for Brown Edge in June 1983. It was formerly London Transport DMS 2128 and came from Ensign Purfleet, with Turner's Daimler Fleetline VBF 799J going in part exchange

The second ex-London Transport Daimler Fleetline purchased by Turner's was OJD 164R (No. 6), seen here arriving into Hanley on 15 September 1982 shortly after arriving in the fleet. These buses reintroduced high-bridge buses into the Turner's fleet. It was new to London Transport as DMS 2164 and also came from Ensign Bus Purfleet with Turner's Daimler Fleetline JRF 446K going in part exchange.

The ex-London Transport Daimler Fleetlines lasted around four years in service with Turner's before being exchanged for two youthful ex-West Yorkshire PTE Roe-bodied Leyland Olympians from Ensign Bus. EWY 78Y (No. 6) is seen in Smallthorne on a sunny summer evening in 1987. These were the first buses in the Turner's fleet to carry three track number blinds, so the Hanley–Brown Edge route was then numbered 49, later changing to 69.

The second ex-West Yorkshire PTE Roe-bodied Leyland Olympian purchased by Turner's was consecutively numbered EWY 79Y (No. 5), seen here leaving the old Hanley bus station in summer 1987. These two Olympians introduced a simplified Turner's livery with just the former green area painted Tudor Maroon and the cream staying the same. They only worked for Turner's for six months before the sale of the company to PMT in October 1987.

Via Travel of Nantwich ventured into Hanley on the once-a-day return journey X81 from Winsford to Hanley. Volvo B10M East Lancs rebody PJI 9173 is seen arriving in Hanley. It was new as a Duple-bodied coach to Western Scottish as NCS 117W in June 1981.

Wardle Transport imported three of these short wheelbase tri-axle Alexander RH-bodied Leyland Olympians from City Bus Hong Kong in 2004 to operate school services and Stoke City FC football buses. K345 OFM carries an all-over advert for Emma Bridgewater Pottery when seen here in Burslem in June 2010. It was formerly registered FS 7204 in Hong Kong as City Bus No. 207.

Three Stoke-on-Trent City Council-owned twelve-seater Optare Alero minibuses were operated by Wardle Transport on demand responsive services around Stoke-on-Trent and carried Stoke-on-Trent Cityrider livery. YP52 BPF is seen at Bradeley when new in October 2002.

Wardle Transport operated six of these Stoke-on-Trent City Council-owned Alexander-bodied Dennis Darts on part-tendered route 62 from Hanley to Tunstall via Milton, Ball Green and Haywood Hospital. DA51 XTE is seen at Ball Green. They had previously operated for D&G Bus in Cityrider livery.

When a spare bus was needed for route 62, Wardle Transport purchased this early Duple Dartline-bodied Dennis Dart G141 GOL (No. 11). It is seen here at Haywood Hospital. This bus was new as a Duple demonstrator and had previously worked locally for Stevensons of Spath.

Wardle Transport also operated some standard two-axle Leyland Olympians such as heavily modified Alexander RL-bodied MNZ 1138, seen here outside the Burslem garage in May 2010. It was new to Merseybus as E219 WBG but has had a former West Midlands Travel Metrobus destination display fitted as well as a modified front panel. It also carries Leyland and Optare badges.

Marshall-bodied Dennis Dart SLF R704 MEW was one of the last buses to enter service with Wardle Transport before the company was sold to Arriva Midlands in 2010. It was new to MTL London as their DMS 4 and is seen at Chell Heath on 20 May 2010.

Wardle Transport also operated two former Nottingham City Transport East Lancs-bodied Volvo Olympians. WBZ 8737, seen here outside the Burslem garage on 24 October 2010 ready to work a Stoke City FC supporters bus, had low-bridge bodywork and was formerly registered P490 CVO. The other ex-Nottingham Olympian, R468 RRA, had high-bridge Pyoneer bodywork.